LÖVE for Lua
Game Programming

Master the Lua programming language and build
exciting strategy-based games in 2D using the
LÖVE framework

Darmie Akinlaja

PUBLISHING

BIRMINGHAM - MUMBAI

LÖVE for Lua Game Programming

First published: September 2013

Second published: October 2013

Production Reference: 2251013

Published by Packt Publishing Ltd.
Livery Place
35 Livery Street
Birmingham B3 2PB, UK.

ISBN 978-1-78216-160-8

www.packtpub.com

Cover Image by Asher Wishkerman (wishkerman@hotmail.com)

Credits

Author

Darmie Akinlaja

Reviewers

Stanislav Costiuc

Alexander Krasij

Acquisition Editor

Akram Hussain

Kartikey Pandey

Commissioning Editor

Harsha Bharwani

Technical Editors

Gaurav Thingalaya

Dennis John

Project Coordinator

Michelle Quadros

Proofreader

Stephen Copestake

Indexer

Monica Ajmera Mehta

Graphics

Valentina Dsilva

Production Coordinator

Kyle Albuquerque

Cover Work

Kyle Albuquerque

About the Author

Darmie Akinlaja is a physicist and software developer who actively develops and contributes to the architecture of RubiQube—a cross-platform mobile application that gives users access to a variety of innovative HTML5 applications based on their location. He serves as the Head of Mobile at MobiQube Ltd., a software company located in the city of Lagos, Nigeria, where he's dedicated to developing rich mobile applications for clients.

In 2008, Darmie supported his college best friend in developing a social network, which enjoyed its moment of fame at the Federal University of Technology, Akure. In 2011, his interest in video games and animations deepened, so he founded a video game production start-up, Gigaware Enterprise, with the goal of creating the best quality and fun games with local African contexts.

Darmie's passion for technology began at the age of 7 when he had his first encounter with a computer system; ever since, his curiosity has helped him discover a lot about technology and also helped him learn everything by himself.

I want to thank my family for believing in me and not giving up on me and on my seemingly stupid dreams and ideas. My love goes to my bestie Deborah Jesutomiwo Elijah for standing by me. I want to thank my great friends Ademola Morebise, Olusola Amusan, and Timilehin Ayekitan; I really appreciate your efforts in rekindling my chutzpah. I am grateful to my employer, MobiQube, for giving me the opportunity to flex my muscles on innovative tasks. And I can never thank God enough for His unfailing grace and love despite all my human efforts.

About the Reviewers

Stanislav Costiuc comes from the town of Beltsy, Moldova. He developed an interest in video games in his early childhood, and at around 9 years old realized that developing them was his profession of choice.

Since then Stanislav studied the ropes of Game Design, Programming, and other game-related disciplines as he worked on mods, collaborative projects on the Internet, and as a freelancer. After graduating from high school he went through Vancouver Film School's Game Design program in Canada and currently works as a Game Designer at Peak Games.

I would like to thank my family and Irina Turtureanu for all their support and encouragement.

Alexander Krasij is a programmer and a minimalist. His work can be found online at www.AlexK.net.

www.PacktPub.com

Support files, eBooks, discount offers and more

You might want to visit www.PacktPub.com for support files and downloads related to your book.

Did you know that Packt offers eBook versions of every book published, with PDF and ePub files available? You can upgrade to the eBook version at www.PacktPub.com and as a print book customer, you are entitled to a discount on the eBook copy. Get in touch with us at service@packtpub.com for more details.

At www.PacktPub.com, you can also read a collection of free technical articles, sign up for a range of free newsletters and receive exclusive discounts and offers on Packt books and eBooks.

http://PacktLib.PacktPub.com

Do you need instant solutions to your IT questions? PacktLib is Packt's online digital book library. Here, you can access, read and search across Packt's entire library of books.

Why Subscribe?
- Fully searchable across every book published by Packt
- Copy and paste, print and bookmark content
- On demand and accessible via web browser

Free Access for Packt account holders

If you have an account with Packt at www.PacktPub.com, you can use this to access PacktLib today and view nine entirely free books. Simply use your login credentials for immediate access.

Table of Contents

Preface

LÖVE is a popular open source 2D video game framework that allows you to leverage the simplicity of the Lua scripting language in developing game prototypes quickly and easily. LÖVE's robustness and active community support make it a viable framework for game development. It has empowered a lot of indie developers of various ages around the world, giving them an edge in tapping into the lucrative video game market.

Its simplicity and "write less build more" nature make it easy for both experienced and novice developers.

This book is a comprehensive tutorial, demonstrating the full potential of LÖVE framework. It takes you through building a prototype to packaging games quickly with LÖVE.

What this book covers

Chapter 1, Getting Started with LÖVE, gets you up-and-running with LÖVE and shows you how to install LÖVE framework and run a LÖVE game.

Chapter 2, LÖving Up!, takes you through drawing a 2D object, moving objects, and animating a game character.

Chapter 3, Before You Build a Game, takes you through the necessary things you need to know before you develop your game.

Chapter 4, Making Your First Game, sets the magic rolling! The chapter will take you through designing and loading a game level, and setting up your game characters and assets.

Chapter 5, More About Making the Game, introduces you to game physics—adding collisions and gravity to game objects—and a more efficient way to animate characters.

Chapter 6, Meeting the Bad Guy!, explains how to set up the enemy character.

Chapter 7, Pickups and Head-Up Display and Sounds, explains how to set up the extras: pickups, sounds, and Head-Up Display (HUD).

Chapter 8, Packaging and Distributing Your Game, explains how to package and distribute our game to various platforms, now that your game is ready to ship.

What you need for this book

To run the examples in the book, the following software will be required:

- Operating systems:
  - Windows XP or above (for Windows users)
  - Ubuntu 10.10 or above (for Linux users)
  - Mac OS X (for Mac users)

- LÖVE framework 0.80 or above (www.love2d.org)
- Tiled Map Editor (www.mapeditor.org)
- Notepad++ Text Editor (www.notepad-plus-plus.org)

Who this book is for

This book is for aspiring game developers with a decent understanding of Lua scripting language, and anyone who wants to learn video game design. If you are looking for a step-by-step approach to learn how to design a game from idea to prototype quickly with a robust and easy-to-understand game engine, this book is for you.

Conventions

In this book, you will find a number of styles of text that distinguish between different kinds of information. Here are some examples of these styles, and an explanation of their meaning.

Code words in text are shown as follows:

"We can configure the screen size and program title using the `love.conf(w)`"

A block of code is set as follows:

```
function love.conf(w)

w.screen.width = 800

w.screen.height = 600

w.screen.title = "Goofy's Adventure"

end
```

A comment within a block of code starts with a double hyphen "--"

When we wish to draw your attention to a particular part of a code block, the relevant lines or items are set in bold:

```
findSolidTiles(map)
   for i, obj in pairs( map("Objects").objects ) do

      if obj.type == "player" then PlayerSpawn(obj.x,obj.y-8) end
      if obj.type == "enemy" then EnemySpawn(obj.x,obj.y-
         14,obj.properties.dir) end
      ---insert items here
      if obj.type == "diamond" then DiamondSpawn(obj.x,obj.y-16) end
      if obj.type == "coins" then CoinSpawn(obj.x,obj.y-16) end

      if obj.type == "life" then LifeSpawn(obj.x,obj.y-16) end

   end
```

Any command-line input or output is written as follows:

```
# cd c:/users/DarmieAkinlaja/My Documents/My game
```

New terms and **important words** are shown in bold. Words that you see on the screen, in menus or dialog boxes for example, appear in the text like this: " for example on my computer, the **My game** folder is stored in **My Documents** folder ".

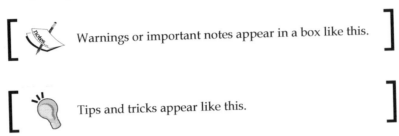

Warnings or important notes appear in a box like this.

Tips and tricks appear like this.

Reader feedback

Feedback from our readers is always welcome. Let us know what you think about this book—what you liked or may have disliked. Reader feedback is important for us to develop titles that you really get the most out of.

To send us general feedback, simply send an e-mail to feedback@packtpub.com, and mention the book title via the subject of your message.

If there is a topic that you have expertise in and you are interested in either writing or contributing to a book, see our author guide on www.packtpub.com/authors.

Customer support

Now that you are the proud owner of a Packt book, we have a number of things to help you to get the most from your purchase.

Downloading the example code

You can download the example code files for all Packt books you have purchased from your account at http://www.packtpub.com. If you purchased this book elsewhere, you can visit http://www.packtpub.com/support and register to have the files e-mailed directly to you.

Errata

Although we have taken every care to ensure the accuracy of our content, mistakes do happen. If you find a mistake in one of our books—maybe a mistake in the text or the code—we would be grateful if you would report this to us. By doing so, you can save other readers from frustration and help us improve subsequent versions of this book. If you find any errata, please report them by visiting http://www.packtpub.com/submit-errata, selecting your book, clicking on the **errata submission form** link, and entering the details of your errata. Once your errata are verified, your submission will be accepted and the errata will be uploaded on our website, or added to any list of existing errata, under the Errata section of that title. Any existing errata can be viewed by selecting your title from http://www.packtpub.com/support.

Piracy

Piracy of copyright material on the Internet is an ongoing problem across all media. At Packt, we take the protection of our copyright and licenses very seriously. If you come across any illegal copies of our works, in any form, on the Internet, please provide us with the location address or website name immediately so that we can pursue a remedy.

Please contact us at copyright@packtpub.com with a link to the suspected pirated material.

We appreciate your help in protecting our authors, and our ability to bring you valuable content.

Questions

You can contact us at questions@packtpub.com if you are having a problem with any aspect of the book, and we will do our best to address it.

Getting Started with LÖVE 1

LÖVE is a fantastic framework that leverages the Lua scripting language for developing 2D games; it is open source, free to use, and licensed under `zlib/libpng`. You can learn more about Lua programming at `www.lua.org`.

In this chapter we'll go through the following:

- All we need to get started with LÖVE
- How to install LÖVE
- How to run a LÖVE game
- Choosing the editors

And a step further to understand the basic structure that makes a LÖVE game.

Downloading LÖVE

Before we build our game, we need a copy of LÖVE's engine running on our computer; a copy of the framework installed will help the computer to interpret the code we will be writing.

Direct your web browser to `www.love2d.org`, scroll to the download section of the site and choose the installer that is compatible with your computer.

It is advisable that we download an installer instead of the source codes, except for when we want to be geeky and build it ourselves.

For Windows users

When you are through with downloading the installer, run the setup and follow the instructions.

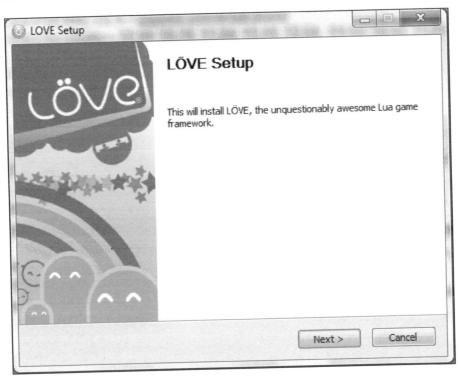

When your installation is complete, run the program; you should see a the window displaying a beautiful animation on the screen.

For Linux users

Linux users are required to download the .deb install file by clicking on build number of their operating system; users running Precise Pangolin Ubuntu OS should click on the **12.04** link. Run the install program and follow the instructions. If the LÖVE framework is fully installed, you can double-click on a .love file to run it.

For Mac users

Mac users should visit the LÖVE wiki (`https://www.love2d.org/wiki/Getting_Started`) page for instructions on how to install LÖVE and run a packaged game.

Choosing your editor

In choosing a suitable editor, you can use any text editor that supports the Lua programming language; we recommend Notepad++; it is free and has a clean and non-confusing GUI.

Running a LÖVE game

First of all, we assume we do not have any LÖVE game yet. OK, then let's just write a simple "Hello World!" program and run it with LÖVE. Open up a text editor and write the following Lua code:

```lua
--create a display

function love.draw()
--display a text on a 800 by 600 screen in the positions x= 400, and
--y=300
    love.graphics.print('hello world!', 400, 300)

end
```

Now save this code as `main.lua`. Open a folder for your game project, put your `main.lua` file inside the folder, and compress the content of the folder. Change the `.zip` extension to `.love`. You'll notice a change in the icon of the compressed file; it changes to a LÖVE logo. Now that we've done all that, we can run our game. If you follow the instructions correctly, you should see a screen similar to the following screenshot:

If you do not compress the file properly, you will get the following blue screen displaying error information:

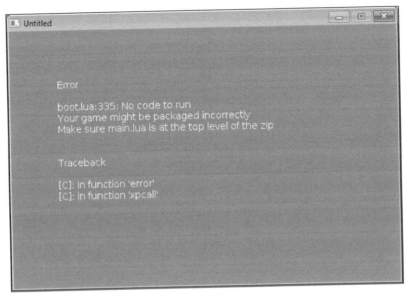

Note that it is the content of your game folder that should be compressed and not the folder itself, and make sure the `main.lua` file is at the top level.

Basic structure of LÖVE

There are three basic functions that make up a LÖVE game that are essential in most of the games you will be designing with LÖVE. For now, the following are the basics to make a small game:

- `love.load()`: This preloads all the necessary assets we need to make our game.
- `love.update(dt)`: This is where we do most of our maths, where we deal with events; it is called before a frame is drawn. `dt` is the time it takes to draw a frame (in seconds).
- `love.draw()`: This draws all that we want to display on the screen.

Examples

The basic structure of the game is done as you can see in the following code:

```
--load our assets
function love.load()
    --load all assets here
end




--update event
function love.update(dt)
--do the maths
end


--draw display
function love.draw()
--describe how you want/what to draw.
end
```

That's just it, well... maybe! So let's play with these chunks one more time.

Now let's edit main.lua to enable loading sample assets that we want to use within the game:

```
function love.load()

    local myfont = love.graphics.newFont(45)

    love.graphics.setFont(myfont)

    love.graphics.setColor(0,0,0,225)

    love.graphics.setBackgroundColor(255,153,0)
end


function love.update()


end
```

```
function love.draw()

    love.graphics.print('Hello World!', 200, 200)

end
```

Conf.lua

Before you go on and start coding your game, you need to give your video game some specs such as window width, window height, and window title. So set up a new file named `conf.lua`; inside it you can then create your game specs as shown in the following code snippet:

```
function love.conf(w)

w.screen.width = 1024

w.screen.height = 768

w.screen.title = "Goofy's Adventure"

end
```

You can manipulate the figures and titles any way and also change that w to whatever variable you want.

The preceding code does the following:

- Loads our font
- Sets the font color
- Sets the background color
- Draws text on the screen
- Configures the screen size

Basically we are using the `love.graphics` module; it can be used to draw (in the real sense) texts, images, and any drawable object in the scene. In the previous code snippets, we defined our fonts with the `love.graphics.newFont(45)` that formats our text by declaring the size of the font as 45. `setFont()` loads the font we defined as `myfont`, `setColor()` colors the text in the RGB format, and `setBackgroundColor()` sets the background.

Then we printed text using the `love.graphics.print('text', x, y)` function in the `draw` function with three parameters parsed in it: the text and the x and y coordinates. We are not going to do anything in the `love.update()` function yet, because we are not dealing with scene events.

So let's load our game as a `.love` file and see what it displays:

Summary

Now we can grab a mug of cappuccino with Ray-Bans on and smile; we have installed the LÖVE game engine, text editor, and Visual tile-level editor (Tiled). We have also got a quick look at the basic structure for writing our game in Lua and displayed "Hello World!" in a colored background window. Next we'll go through how to draw 2D objects, move objects, and animate character sprites.

2
LÖving Up!

Now, let's have fun with LÖVE. We'll do the following in this chapter:

- Draw objects
- Move them around
- Animate characters
- Discuss sprites

Drawing 2D objects

LÖVE's `love.graphics` module already has in-built functions for drawing specific shapes such as a circle, arc, and rectangle. So let's draw all these shapes in a single game. Create a new game folder, rename it as `shapes`, open a new `main.lua` file in this directory, and edit it by adding the following code:

```
function love.load() ---loads all we need in game

--- set color for our shapes RGB

    love.graphics.setColor(0, 0, 0, 225)

--- set the background color RGB

    love.graphics.setBackgroundColor(225, 153, 0)

end

function love.draw() ---function to display/draw content to screen

---draw circle with parameters(mode, x-pos, y-pos, radius, segments)
```

```
        love.graphics.circle("fill", 200, 300, 50, 50)

    ---draw rectangle with parameters(mode, x-pos, y-pos, width, height)

        love.graphics.rectangle("fill", 300, 300, 100, 100)

    ---draw an arc with parameters(mode,x-pos,y-pos,radius,angle1,angle2)

        love.graphics.arc("fill", 450, 300, 100, math.pi/5, math.pi/2)



    end
```

By following the comments in the preceding code snippet, we can draw the shapes by using the needed parameters, as shown in the following screenshot:

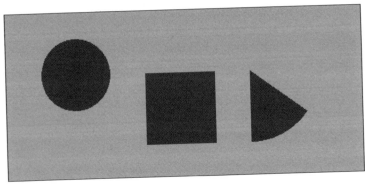

Moving objects

In our game we would want objects to move, rotate, or just change position. That's the essence of a 2D game. So we are going to move an object across the screen and also are going to rotate it.

Rotating objects

We will create a 10 x 10 square and specify the rotation angle as 0 using the `love.graphics.rotate()` function; what the code will do is make the object rotate with keyboard actions. The Boolean `love.keyboard.isDown()` function is used to make keyboard inputs do certain things. Just to cause the object to rotate, we will make the rotation angle increase or decrease in delta time. `math.pi` is the angular speed, which means that the object will rotate at an angular speed of 180 degrees. Replace the previous code with the next code snippet.

First of all, we can define our variables for the angle, width, and height. A **variable** is a name or an identifier for a place in the computer's memory where dynamic content is stored; variables store information that will be used later in the code:

```lua
--variables
local angle = 0

local width = 10

local height = 10

--draw a rectangle
function love.draw()

    -- rotate

    love.graphics.rotate(angle)

    -- draw a blue rectangle

    love.graphics.setColor(0,0,225)

    love.graphics.rectangle('fill', 300, 400, width, height)
end
--update
function love.update(dt)

--- On pressing the 'd' key, rotate to the right

    if love.keyboard.isDown('d') then

    angle = angle + math.pi * dt

--- else if we press the 'a' key, rotate to the left

    elseif love.keyboard.isDown('a') then

    angle = angle - math.pi * dt
    end

end
```

Moving left, right, up, or down

In the next example, we'll cause our character to move left, right, up, or down as a response to keyboard inputs. Before we make a character move, it is advisable to create a table for the character, because some of the character properties might be changed as we play the game. Basically, the property of the character that we intend to change progressively is the position of the object in the x and y axis. Similar to how we made the character rotate in the previous example, we will make the x and y positions of the character change on keyboard input. The position of the object is updated just by a simple increment $x = x + 1$ or $y = y + 1$. The initial position of the object (in x and y coordinates) will be defined in the code example, then we'll multiply the number of increment 1 by dt for the computer to render the movement in delta time (this is the time your computer will take to render a frame; more about delta time will be discussed later).

```
function love.load()

--- create a character table, our character is a rectangle, the
initial position of the character object in the x and y coordinate is
defined in the table as 300 and 400 respectively

character = {}
character.x = 300
character.y = 400

love.graphics.setBackgroundColor(225, 153, 0)

-- paint character blue

love.graphics.setColor(0, 0, 225)

end

function love.draw()

--- draw character
    love.graphics.rectangle("fill", character.x, character.y, 100,
100)


end

function love.update(dt)

--- On pressing the 'd' key, move to the right
```

```
    if love.keyboard.isDown('d') then
-- the increment value can be changed depending on how far you want
the object to go in single press of the button
        character.x = character.x + 1 * dt

--- else if we press the 'a' key, move to the left

    elseif love.keyboard.isDown('a') then

    character.x = character.x - 1 * dt
    end
--- if we press the 'W' key, move to the up
if love.keyboard.isDown('w') then

    character.y = character.y - 1 * dt

--- else if we press the 'S' key, move to the down

elseif love.keyboard.isDown('s') then

    character.y = character.y + 1 * dt
    end

end
```

The following is the output:

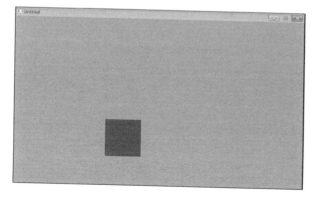

Now try and run your game using the WASD keys to move the blue square about.

Sprites

Let's briefly discuss sprites. In gaming, **sprites** are usually used for animation sequences; a sprite is a single image in which individual frames of a character animation are stored. We are going use sprites in our animations.

If you already have knowledge of graphics design, it's good for you because it is an edge for you to define how you want your game to look like and how you want to define animation sequences in sprites. You can try out tools such as Sprite Maker for making your own sprites with ease; you can get a copy of Sprite Maker at `http://www.spriteland.com/sprites/sprite-maker.zip`.

The following is an sample animation sprite by Marc Russell, which is available for free at `http://opengameart.org/content/gfxlib-fuzed` you can find other open source sprites at `http://opengameart.org/content/platformersidescroller-tiles`:

The preceding sprite will play the animation of the character moving to the right. The character sequence is well organized using an invisible grid, as shown in the following screenshot:

The grid is 32 x 32; the size of our grid is very important in setting up the quads for our game. A **quad** in LÖVE is a specific part of an image. Because our sprite is a single image file, quads will be used to specify each of the sequences we want to draw per unit time and will be the largest part part of our animation algorithm.

Animation

The animation algorithm will simply play the sprite like a tape of film; we'll be using a basic technique here as LÖVE doesn't have an official module for that. Some members of the LÖVE forum have come up with different libraries to ease the way we play animations. The use of animation libraries will come up in later chapters. First of all let us load our file:

```
function love.load()

    sprite = love.graphics.newImage "sprite.png"

end
```

Then we create quads for each part of the sprite by using `love.graphics.newQuad(x, y, width, height, sw, sh)`, where x is the top-left position of the quad along the x axis, y is the top-left position of the quad along the y axis, `width` is the width of the quad, `height` is the height of the quad, `sw` is the sprite's width, and `sh` is the sprite's height:

```
love.graphics.newQuad(0, 0, 32, 32, 256, 32) --- first quad

    love.graphics.newQuad(32, 0, 32, 32, 256, 32) --- second quad

    love.graphics.newQuad(64, 0, 32, 32, 256, 32) --- Third quad

    love.graphics.newQuad(96, 0, 32, 32, 256, 32) --- Fourth quad

    love.graphics.newQuad(128, 0, 32, 32, 256, 32) --- Fifth quad

    love.graphics.newQuad(160, 0, 32, 32, 256, 32) --- Sixth quad

    love.graphics.newQuad(192, 0, 32, 32, 256, 32) --- Seventh quad

    love.graphics.newQuad(224, 0, 32, 32, 256, 32) --- Eighth quad
```

The preceding code can be rewritten in a more concise loop as shown in the following code snippet:

```
for i=1,8 do
    love.graphics.newQuad((i-1)*32, 0, 32, 32, 256, 32)
end
```

As advised by LÖVE, we shouldn't state our quads in the `draw()` or `update()` functions, because it will cause the quad data to be repeatedly loaded into memory with every frame, which is a bad practice. So what we'll do is pretty simple; we'll load our quad parameters in a table, while `love.graphics.newQuad` will be referenced locally outside the functions. So the new code will look like the following for the animation in the right direction:

```
local Quad = love.graphics.newQuad

function love.load()

sprite = love.graphics.newImage "sprite.png"

    quads = {}
```

```
    quads['right'] ={}
    quads['left'] = {}
    for j=1,8 do
        quads['right'][j] = Quad((j-1)*32, 0, 32, 32, 256, 32);
        quads['left'][j] = Quad((j-1)*32, 0, 32, 32, 256, 32);
-- for the character to face the opposite direction, the quad need to
be flipped by using the Quad:flip(x, y) method, where x and why are
Boolean.
        quads.left[j]:flip(true, false) --flip horizontally x = true, y
= false

    end
end
```

Now that our animation table is set, it is important that we set a Boolean value for the state of our character. At the start of the game our character is idle, so we set `idle` to `true`. Also, there are a number of quads the algorithm should read in order to play our animation. In our case, we have eight quads, so we need a maximum of eight iterations, as shown in the following code snippet:

```
local Quad = love.graphics.newQuad

function love.load()

character= {}
character.player = love.graphics.newImage("sprite.png")
character.x = 50
character.y = 50
direction = "right"
iteration = 1

max = 8

idle = true
timer = 0.1
    quads = {}
    quads['right'] ={}
    quads['left'] = {}
    for j=1,8 do
        quads['right'][j] = Quad((j-1)*32, 0, 32, 32, 256, 32);
        quads['left'][j] = Quad((j-1)*32, 0, 32, 32, 256, 32);
-- for the character to face the opposite direction, the quad need to
be flipped by using the Quad:flip(x, y) method, where x and why are
Boolean.
        quads.left[j]:flip(true, false) --flip horizontally x = true, y
= false
    end
end
```

Now let us update our motion; if a certain key is pressed, the animation should play; if the key is released, the animation should stop. Also, if the key is pressed, the character should change position. We'll be using the `love.keypressed` callback function here, as shown in the following code snippet:

```
function love.update(dt)

    if idle == false then

        timer = timer + dt
        if timer > 0.2 then
            timer = 0.1
-- The animation will play as the iteration increases, so we just
write iteration = iteration + 1, also we'll stop reset our iteration
at the maximum of 8 with a timer update to keep the animation smooth.
            iteration = iteration + 1
            if love.keyboard.isDown('right') then
                sprite.x = sprite.x + 5
            end
    if love.keyboard.isDown('left') then
                sprite.x = sprite.x - 5
            end
            if iteration > max then

                iteration = 1
            end
        end
    end
end

function love.keypressed(key)

    if quads[key] then
        direction = key
        idle = false
    end
end

function love.keyreleased(key)

    if quads[key] and direction == key then

        idle = true

        iteration = 1

        direction = "right"

    end
end
```

Finally, we can draw our character on the screen. Here we'll be using `love.graphics.drawq(image, quad, x, y)`, where `image` is the image data, `quad` will load our `quads` table, `x` is the position in x axis and `y` is the position in the y axis:

```
function love.draw()

    love.graphics.drawq(sprite.player, quads[direction][iteration],
sprite.x,
sprite.y)

end
```

So let's package our game and run it to see the magic in action by pressing the left or right navigation key:

Summary

That is all for this chapter. We have learned how to draw 2D objects on the screen and move the objects in four directions. We we delved into the usage of sprites for animations and how to play these animations with code. In the next chapter we will learn what we need to know in making our first game.

Before You Build a Game

3

In designing a video game there are a few things you must know. You cannot just wake up one morning and say, "Yeah! I want to make a game". Developing a game is much more like building a house. To build a house, you need a plan and the necessary materials ready.

Before you start, you should ask yourself, "How good is my geometry?" "Do I have a fair understanding of physics?" "Can I code enough?" If yes, yes, and yes, you are good to go! And if no, you should take your time to study and understand the basics of displacement (`http://wikipedia.org/wiki/displacement`), speed (`en.wikipdia.org/wiki/velocity`), and the application of coordinate geometry (`http://www.math.com/school/subject3/lessons/S3U1L2GL.html`).

Since we are considering 2D games, we should be more concerned about the x and y axes of our game objects; the z coordinate is out of the question because we we will only need to refer to that in 3D.

Planning your game

The concept of two-dimensional game is putting all objects in a plane; the z coordinate represents depth, which will not be considered in this scope. Knowing this, all your game graphics are expected to be on a plane, where the x axis and y axis are only considered. Your game objects can move up, left, down, right, in diagonals, and at angles within the x and y coordinates.

What's the idea? How will the game be played? You may want it to be in the isometric view (`http://wikipedia.org/wiki/isometric_projection`) or like a side-scroll, in which the game world presented perpendicular to the direction the characters are facing on the screen. The examples of side-scrolling can be found at `http://www.giantbomb.com/side-scrolling/3015-299/games/`.

Who's playing your game? You can start with your friends and build a game they'll love to play. What genre is your game? You should be able to define what genre your game is; your game can be a combination of one or more genres. Below are the video game genres we have today:

- Strategy
- Role-playing game
- Adventure
- Action
- Simulation

Strategy

This kind of game requires skills, careful reasoning, and planning to achieve the desired victory. In most strategy games, the player's decisions will determine what's next.

Role-playing games

Role-playing video games (commonly referred to as RPGs) are a video game genre where the player controls the actions of a protagonist, as this character lives in an open world. Common RPGs are based on the dungeon and monster concept; the character plays his way through dungeons and gets to fight a monster (usually a dragon).

Adventure

This genre involves the player playing the role of a protagonist, where he interacts with the virtual environment based on a story or role. This usually involves puzzle-like encounters.

Action

This emphasizes physical challenges, which may include fighting, shooting, pick objects, and avoid obstacles. This usually involves quick reflexes, accuracy, and timing to overcome obstacles.

Simulation

This is a genre of game that involves the simulation of real-life objects in a virtual world. For example, you can build a simulation game for flying a jet or driving a car.

Summary

Now that we have learned what we need to know to build our first game, in the next chapter we'll learn how to design our game.

4
Making Your First Game

Now we can design our game world. In this chapter, we'll do the following:

- Create a tile map
- Import our tile set
- Set up edit layers
- Export the final product

Basic level design

Before you begin level design on your computer, you should sketch the level layout—a draft of what the full design may look like. For example, we can sketch a simple level for a platformer game; this example is based on a jungle with many rocky platforms. The player is going to be picking coins and diamonds and also avoiding antagonists.

Then, with whatever computer graphics tool available, you can transfer your sketch to the computer and color it into a more attractive design. (The current design is based on the open-source platformer game assets provided at `http://opengameart.org/content/gfxlib-fuzed`).

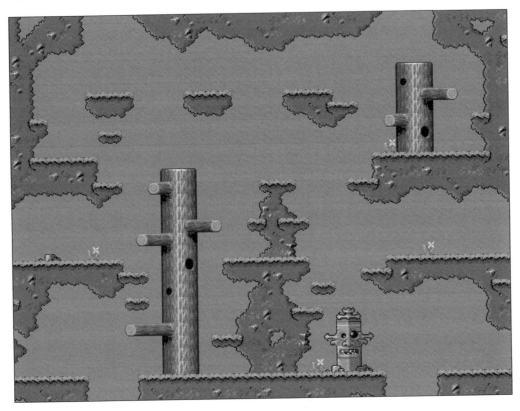

And the following screenshot shows what my final game should look like with a few edits, coins, diamonds, and antagonists:

Getting your assets ready

Having all your assets ready is very important, which includes all the sprites you will need and the tile set of your level. The tile set design is just a fragmentation of the finished sketch you made previously; breaking them into jigsaw-like pieces is necessary for you to design your game level with Tiled.

Player

The sprite of the player with several poses towards the east can be flipped to the opposite direction using `Quad:flip`, as demonstrated in the previous chapter:

Coin

The following is a sprite of coins with several poses so that we can animate it to rotate:

Antagonist

Hey, meet the bad guy. His sprite given here can be used to make him pace about a specific region within the game world:

Diamond

Similar to the coin, the diamond sprite is designed to glitter. The glittering effect can be achieved by animating it. (The animation of coins and diamonds will be done later):

Tile set

The following screenshot shows a tile of images that can be arranged with the Tiled Map Editor (a guide on how to use the Tiled Map Editor can be seen later) to form a game world the way we imagine it—like a jigsaw puzzle!

Getting started with Tiled

Get a copy of Tiled from `http://www.mapeditor.org/` and run `the` Tiled program because before we go ahead; you need to check that your settings are correct (navigate to **Tiled | Preferences**). I recommend the **Base64** encoding, because it produces a smaller file; this makes your game load faster:

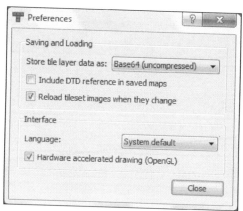

Now open a new file in Tiled, select **Orthogonal**, and choose your preferred width and height for the tile size. We'll be using the 16 x 16 tile size in this example. The level design will be scaled to screen while playing:

Load your tile set by navigating to **Tiled | Map | New Tileset** and selecting your preferred tile set (note that your sprites and tiles must be in the root folder of our game). Select and place the respective tiles in the grids while designing the game level:

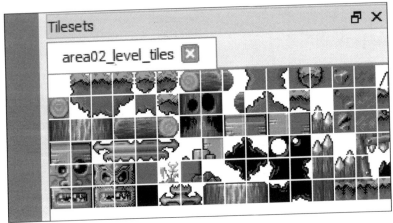

Because we now have our tile set ready, select and place each tile in the respective grid till we form the design we imagined.

The following screenshot shows the surfaces that we would want our player or any moving object to collide with. It is necessary to set up a collision layer so that we can differentiate the collidable part (which the player or other characters will collide with) from the other parts that the player will not collide with:

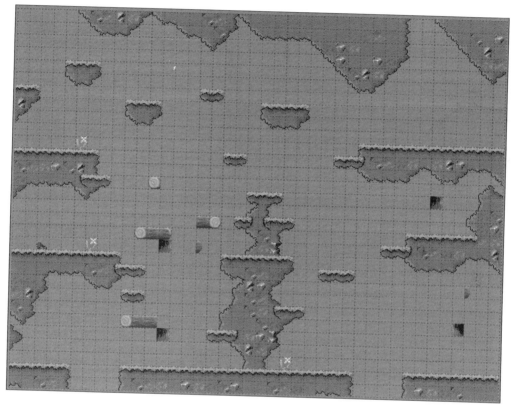

We can go ahead and design layer 2, which is the part the player will not collide with. To create a new layer, navigate to **Tiled | Layer | Add Layer**:

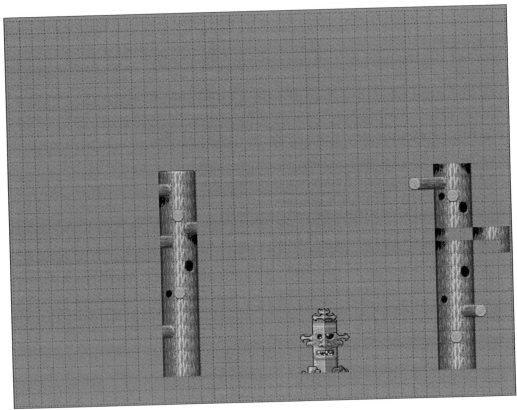

Now that we have layer 2, we should also put the jungle shadow, which is the third layer; each of the layers will be referenced in our game. If the layers are placed on top of each other, we'll have the almost-complete design ready. But to give our players a nice experience with the game, we may have to put in some background layers too, such as the deep dark forest feature. It should take just an hour to finish the whole design.

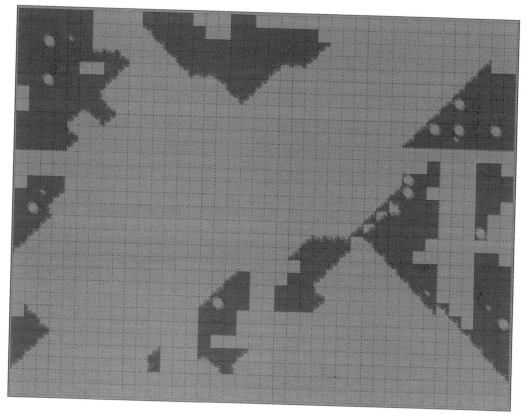

The following is the deep dark forest background that we would add to our game:

You can add the preceding background using the following lines of code:

```
bg = love.graphics.newImage("background.png") function love.draw()
    love.graphics.draw(bg)
end
```

By bringing it all together; we can have an almost complete view of our game world. Pretty neat, isn't it?

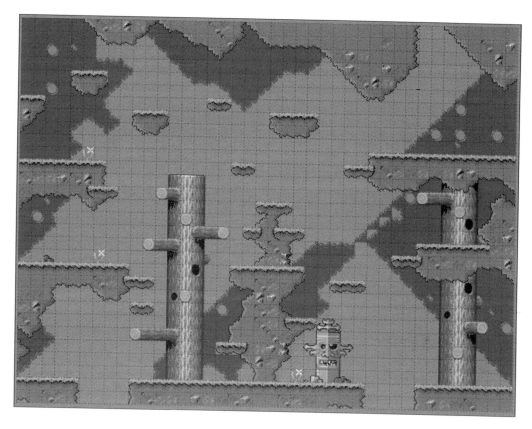

Exporting your tile map

To export our design (tile map), we'll simply click on the **Save as** menu under the **Edit** tab, name the map, and save it in .tmx format. We chose the .tmx format because it's the format the Advanced Tiled Map will be working with. Make sure the exported .tmx file is in the root folder with your other game assets.

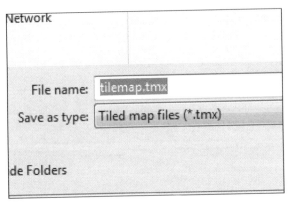

Loading the game level

Advanced Tiled Loader is an open source script (concept), and can be found on GitHub at https://github.com/Kadoba/Advanced-Tiled-Loader. Download it, decompress it, and put the Advanced-Tiled-Loader-master folder in the source directory of your game. Then create a maps directory and place your exported .tmx file (tile map file) and the tile sprite image (we want to assume you designed your game level from this directory, else your game might return some errors) in it. So the script to load our tile map is as follows:

```
--platformer with TILED


local loader = require ("Advanced-Tiled-Loader-master/Loader")

---the path to our .tmx files and sprites

loader.path = "maps/"

function love.load()

    love.graphics.setBackgroundColor(225, 153, 0)

-- load the level and bind the variable map

    map = loader.load("tilemap.tmx")
```

```
    end

    function love.draw()

        map:draw()

    end
```

That's it. Now you can run your game and see; it's that simple. You should see your level design display as you did it. We might have to resize the window frame to fit our game.

Conf.lua

For the tile map we just designed, it is necessary that we change the screen configuration to match it. The following is the new config.lua file:

```
    function love.conf(w)

        w.screen.width = 640

        w.screen.height = 480

        w.title = "Goofy's Adventure"

    end
```

Summary

And that's it! Now that we have done this, we'll continue with adding collision callback to tiles and other objects in the game in the next chapter.

5

More About Making the Game

We have learned how to use the Tiled program and design our game level. Now we'll learn how to load our tiled level design within the game using the **Advanced TiledMap Loader (ATL)** and add collisions using the `bump.lua` library by Kikito.

In this chapter, we'll learn how to do the following:

- Add collisions to tiles and objects
- Load the player and enemy into the game world
- Add a gravitational force

We'll also learn a new and quicker method of animating the characters by using the `anim8` library.

Bump on it!

This is where we'll configure our collision system using the `bump.lua` library. `bump.lua` is a lightweight library that can be found at `http://github.com/kikito/bump.lua`. Let's edit our previous code and set up the bump. We'll also set up our player to move within the solid world and collide with it. It's a long chunk, so you need to follow the comments to understand what each chunk does!

1. First of all we require the bump library within `main.lua`:

```
bump = require "bump"
```

2. Next, we define our collision callback function `bump.collision()`, between two objects:

```
function bump.collision(obj1, obj2, dx, dy)
```

3. Then we define the conditions for a collision between the two objects:

```
function bump.shouldCollide(obj1, obj2)
```

4. With this, we get an object and return its collision boundary, which is usually a rectangle of parameters l, t, w, and h:

```
function bump.getBBox(obj)
    return obj.l, obj.t, obj.w, obj.h
end
```

We'll come back and fill the blank spaces between these chunks after we have loaded our solid tiles and objects (characters).

Loading solid tiles into the bump

Now we are going to fetch all the solid tiles/layers and make them respond to collision. We'll do this by the using the `FindSolidTiles()` function; but first we'll load the tiles from Tiled with `LoadTiledMap(levelFile)` which will later override `map = loader.load()` that we already defined; this is because we want our bumped tiles to load when the tile map loads:

```
    --our tiles are 16x16 sizes, so we should declare the width and
height as 16
    local tWidth = 16
    local tHeight = 16
function LoadTileMap(levelFile)
    map = loader.load(levelFile)
    FindSolidTiles(map)
--set this to false, will be made true later on.
    map.drawObjects = false
end

---create a table to hold all the solid tiles, you can call it blocks

blocks = {}
---from the layer labelled "platform" within tiled, we call the layer
and strip out all the tiles,
function FindSolidTiles(map)
    layer = map.layers["platform"]
-- get the width and height of each and set them inside the
    for tileX=1,map.width do
        for tileY=1,map.height do
            local tile = layer(tileX-1, tileY-1)
            if tile then

---set the rectangle of the tiles, l, t, w and h parameters and make
```

```
static and collidable

            local block = {l=(tileX-1)*16,t=(tileY-1)*16,w= tWidth,h=
tHeight }

            blocks[#blocks+1] = block
            ---make solid tiles collidable
            bump.addStatic(block)
        end
      end
    end
end
```

Loading the character objects (player and enemy)

Character objects must be first loaded within the Tiled program by creating an object layer. You can do this by performing the following steps:

1. Click on **Layer** and select **Add Object Layer**.

2. On the right-hand side pane, rename the layer as `Characters`.

3. Then import the tile sets/sprites of our characters by clicking on **Map**, then selecting **New Tileset**, and then importing the tile set as shown in the following screenshot:

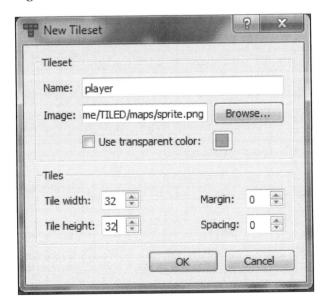

Be sure of the size of each cell in the sprite, as shown in the preceding screenshot. The sprite cell size is 32 x 32. We can now place the objects in the preferred position. After you place the object, right-click on it and set the object property (the type is either enemy or player) for our player, as shown in the following screenshot:

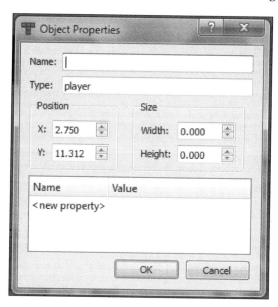

We can follow the same set of instructions for the enemy:

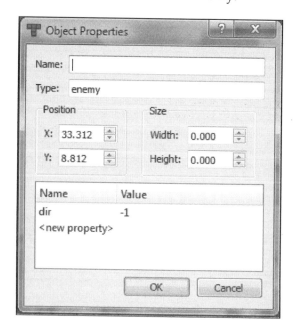

Set the type as `enemy`, create a value of `-1`, and give it a name `dir` on the table, as seen in the preceding screenshot. This is because we'll be calling on the enemy character to know which direction it's taking while it moves in a loop.

Now we'll define the player and enemy entities in chunks of code: what they'll do, how they'll interact, and also make them collidable with bump.

A player character

The player character will be doing simple things such as killing the enemy, jumping, and walking towards the left or right, making it spawn, and also colliding with the platform.

```
---set the player's collider box left, Right and height spaces

playerCollideboxL = 8

playerCollideboxR = 8

playerCollideboxY = 4
```

The player spawn function binds the collider with the player's `left`, `right`, and `height` space parameters. Our player is size 32:

```
function PlayerSpawn(x,y)

    local left = x + playerCollideboxL
    local right = 32
    local height = 32 - playerCollideboxY
```

1. Create a table to hold all the player's necessary properties:

```
player = {}
player.name="player"

---player left
player.l=x

--player bottom space

player.t=y+playerCollideboxY

--player right space

player.w=right

--player height
player.h=height
```

```
--current layer's velocity (vY) in the Y axis
player.vY=0
--player's current direction

player.dir=1
```

2. Add `player` to `bump`, so the player can collide too:

```
bump.add(player)

--where's the player, up or down?
IsOnGround = false

IsJumping = false

JumpRel = true

end
```

The anim8 library

We have already set up our player and collider box; the `player` object is now collidable, but we need to animate it. Earlier on, we already created animation with quad (*Chapter 2, LÖving Up!*). Now we'll be using a cleaner and straightforward animation library—**anim8** (`love2D.org/wiki/anim8`). Just as with the bump library and ATL, we are also going to require the `anim8` library in `main.lua`; be sure that you have already downloaded a copy of the library for use and make sure `anim8.lua` is in the same directory with `main.lua`.

```
anim8 = require "anim8"
```

1. Set the player character sprite, the same one we loaded in Tiled as the `player` object:

```
playerSprite = love.graphics.newImage("maps/sprite.png")
```

2. Set up the character's grid and size (`playerSprite:getWidth()` and `playerSprite:getHeight()`)"

```
local a8 = anim8.newGrid(32,32,playerSprite:getWidth(),
playerSprite:getHeight())
```

3. Now let's define our animation states:

```
playerWalkRight = anim8.newAnimation('loop', a8('1-8',1), 0.1)
playerJumpRight = anim8.newAnimation('loop', a8(4,1), 0.1)
playerIdleRight = anim8.newAnimation('loop', a8(1,1), 0.1)

playerWalkLeft = anim8.newAnimation('loop', a8('1-
```

```
8',1),0.1,nil,true)

playerJumpLeft = anim8.newAnimation('loop', a8(4,1), 0.1,nil,true)

playerIdleLeft = anim8.newAnimation('loop', a8(1,1), 0.1,nil,true)
```

The preceding function, `anim8.newAnimation()`, holds the parameters mode, frames, default delay, delays, and flip in the syntax `anim8.newAnimation (mode, frames, defaultDelay, delay, flippedV, flippedH)` and creates a new animation.

Frames

Frames can be easily declared with the grid by building groups of quads of the same size. To do this we need to define the size of each strip of the character in a sprite and also the size of the whole sprite itself. That is what we have defined previously in `anim8.newGrid()`. It's a convenient way of getting frames from sprites. The frames are like cells of a different pose of the character sprite and are distributed in columns such that frame (1, 1) is the one in the first row and in the first column. From what we did in `a8('1-8', 1)`, we get the previous row of eight elements; that is, we want the animation to be played through the eight columns of the sprite.

Animation

Animations are group of frames interchanged through a row in a sprite over and over again. It is written in the form `anim8.newAnimation(mode, frames, defaultDelay, delays, flippedV, flippedH)`, where the `mode` of the animation can be `loop`, `once`, or `bounce`.

- `loop`: In this mode, the animation can play through the frame; when it reaches the last, it starts all over again
- `once`: In this mode, the animation gets repeated just once and stays on the last frame until it is reset
- `bounce`: In this mode, as you might have predicted, the animation plays till the last frame, but this time doesn't start over from the first; it just plays the animation backwards and goes forward again

The `delays` value is optional; it specifies the individual delay of frames—the lag before the next frame is played. `flippedV` and `flippedH` are used to determine if we want our animation to flip vertically or horizontally.

Player movement

We already set up our animation states but the player has to move while being animated. When we move the player to any direction, the animation will play along in delta time. The player will also be responding to keyboard inputs such as WASD:

```
function PlayerMovement(dt)
local speed = 100

IsOnGround = false
    if (love.keyboard.isDown("up") or love.keyboard.isDown("x")) then
```

1. Check whether the player is on the ground:

```
        if (IsOnGround == true) then
            --be sure the jump key is not being held down

            if JumpRel then
```

2. Set the value of the initial jump force to that of the jump acceleration:

```
            JumpForce = JumpAccel
```

3. Set the y velocity to the jump force value:

```
            player.vY = JumpForce
```

4. Ensure that the player is jumping; we use the following line of code:

```
            IsJumping = true
```

5. If the jump key is held down:

```
                JumpRel = false
                JumpTimer = 0.065
            end
        else
```

6. Check whether the player is jumping and whether the jump key is being held down:

```
        if (IsJumping) and (JumpRel == false) then
            if (JumpTimer > 0) then
    --- push player upwards
                JumpForce = JumpForce + JumpAccel * dt
                player.vY = JumpForce
            end
        end
    end
end
```

7. If we press left key:

```
if love.keyboard.isDown('left') then

--move player and animate it to the left
    player.l = player.l - speed * dt
    playAnimation = playerWalkLeft
    player.dir = -1
```

8. Else move and animate player to the right if the right key pressed:

```
elseif love.keyboard.isDown('right') then
    player.l = player.l + speed * dt
    playAnimation = playerWalkRight
    player.dir = 1
```

9. Set idle states if player's direction is greater than zero:

```
else
    if (player.dir > 0) then playAnimation = playerIdleRight

    else playAnimation = playerIdleLeft end
end
```

10. Update the animation sequence in delta time:

```
playAnimation:update(dt)
---if the player is not jumping remain at ground zero
if not IsJumping then
    JumpForce = 0
end
```

11. If the player falls in a canal, the player has fallen off the tile map; this means that the height between the player's bottom and the ground is greater than the height of the tile map, so the player dies:

```
if (player.t > map.height*16) then Die() end
---when the player jumps, and the timer is greater than zero,
suspend the player on air for sometime before drop
    if (JumpTimer > 0) then
        JumpTimer = JumpTimer - dt
    end

end
```

Gravitation physics

When the jump key is pressed, we want the player to jump and land (respond to gravity); the player will be displaced in space `player.t` at the velocity of `player.vY`. The value of `player.t` and `player.vY` will increase while travelling northwards and reduce when travelling southwards, but first let's set up our gravitation physics. In Tiled, edit the property of your tile map, click on **Map**, select **Map Properties**, and set an empty field for gravity. Then update the `LoadTileMap()` function to fetch the `map` property for gravity:

```
function LoadTileMap(levelFile)
    map = loader.load(levelFile)
---set gravity to 1000
    gravity = 1000


    FindSolidTiles(map)
    ---since we have setup player property in previous chunk, fetch
player object and let it spawn to position

for i, obj in pairs( map("Characters").objects ) do

    if obj.type == "player" then PlayerSpawn(obj.x,obj.y-8) end

    end

    map.drawObjects = false

end
```

Now let's make the player drop when it jumps. Add the following code to the `PlayerMovement(dt)` chunk:

```
---the gravitational pull
--There is an increment in the upward movement of the player
    player.vY = player.vY + gravity*dt/2

--also the space between the bottom of our player, player.t increases
with respect to the velocity player.vY

    player.t = player.t + (player.vY * dt)
```

So let us create the jump callback when the up or X key is pressed and released in a separate chunk:

```
function love.keyreleased(k)

--the moment you push the key and then release it perform the jump

    if k=="up" then JumpRel = true end

    if k=="x" then JumpRel = true end
end
```

Player collision with platform

The impact of the player with the platform should be equal and opposite; when the player hits a tile, it is displaced slightly, the incremental change in the motion of the player in x axis (dx) should be negative when the player hits a wall, thereby stopping it or displacing it in the opposite direction.

Thus we update the `bump.collision()` function set in our bump configuration:

```
function bump.collision(obj1, obj2, dx, dy)
```

1. If the first object to collide is the player, the second object is displaced:

```
    if obj1 == player then

        collidePlayerWithPlatform(dx,dy,obj2)
```

2. Else, if the first object happens to be the platform and the second is the player, displace in the opposite direction:

```
    elseif obj2 == player then

        collidePlayerWithPlatform(-dx,-dy,obj1)
    end
end
```

3. Set the collision behavior:

```
    function collidePlayerWithPlatform(dx, dy, obj)

    ---the block is already a static bump, now set the object on
    collision as the block

    local block = obj

    --if the displacement isn't upwards and the block is below the
```

player, then the player is still on the ground and not jumping

```
    if ((dy < 0) and (obj.t > player.t)) then

        IsOnGround = true

        IsJumping = false

        player.vY = 0

---else if the player position is up
    elseif (dy > 0) then

        player.vY = 0
    end
```

4. Change position with respect to the direction of the displacement:

```
    player.l = player.l + dx
    player.t = player.t + dy

    end
```

Player's death

So what happens when our hero dies? He respawns (that means his position resets) or his life cells reduce:

```
---for now make the player re-spawn to position 32,32 on the tilemap
when it dies.
function Die()

    player.l = 32

    player.t = 32
end
```

Draw player

That's it! We got our player fully set up; now let's draw our player to display:

```
function DrawPlayer()
---draw the player sprite in the collide box
--playAnimation:Draw(image, X, Y)
playAnimation:draw(playerSprite,player.l-playerCollideboxL, player.t-
playerCollideboxY)
    end
```

Now we can update our `love.draw()` chunk to draw the player in LÖVE:

```
function love.draw()

    map:draw()

    DrawPlayer()
end
```

Summary

Whew! That was a whole lot, loading the tile map, adding physics (collision and gravity), and player animations; quite technical compared with the previous chapters but clean enough. In the next chapter, we'll set up the antagonist and how it will interact with other objects in the game world.

6

Meeting the Bad Guy!

Now let's set up the antagonist. The bad guy's job is easy; he'll be placed at certain posts and just moves to and fro, like a guard. When the player collides with the enemy, he dies! But when the player jumps on top of the enemy, the enemy dies! You know, just as with the regular NES Super Mario.

Bad guy

We'll define the bad guy's properties; these include his spawn point, direction of motion, and speed of movement.

```
--the enemy table holds all the parameter we need for the enemy's
movement
enemyTable = {}
--length
enemyTable.l=0
--space between the bottom and the ground
enemyTable.t=0
--width
enemyTable.w=32
--height
enemyTable.h=32
--direction
enemyTable.dir=-1
--initial velocity in x direction
enemyTable.vX = 0
--animation state based on direction
enemyTable.animation = EnemyLeft
---set speed and death/life Boolean
local EnemySpeed = 25
local EnemyDied = false
--get the enemy sprite image file
local enemyImage =
```

```
          love.graphics.newImage("maps/wheelie_right.png")

   ---configure animation for enemy
   local a8 = anim8.newGrid(32, 32, enemyImage:getWidth(),
     enemyImage:getHeight())
   local EnemyRight = anim8.newAnimation( a8('1-4',1), 0.9)
   local EnemyLeft = anim8.newAnimation(a8('1-4',1),),0.9,nil,true)
   ---now the EnemySpawn() function, this basically holds the
     parameters to update the enemy's position and to and fro
     movement.
   function EnemySpawn(x,y,dir)
   --for multiple enemies
     local id = #enemyTable+1

     enemyTable[id] = {
       name="enemy",
       --position of enemy grid box from the left

       l=x,
       -- the space between the platform and buttom of the enemy
         character
       t=math.floor(y/16)*16+4,
       --width of the enemy collider
       w=18,
       --height of the enemy collider
       h=32,
       --direction of motion
       dir=dir,
       vX=0,
       animation=EnemyLeft,

       dead = false

     }
     ---add enemy to the bump, to make it collide with platform
   bump.add(enemyTable[id])
   end
```

Updating the enemy position and animation

The enemy's position and animation need constant update. First, we have to know the enemy's current state (dead or alive). If the enemy is alive, update the position and play animation; if not, don't.

First of all, add the enemy information to the list of solid tiles in
`FindSolidTiles(map)`:

```
function LoadTileMap(levelFile)
  map = loader.load(levelFile)
---set gravity to 1000
  gravity = 1000


  FindSolidTiles(map)
  ---list all solid tiles
  for i, obj in pairs( map("Characters").objects ) do

    if obj.type == "player" then PlayerSpawn(obj.x,obj.y-8) end
    if obj.type == "enemy" then EnemySpawn(obj.x,obj.y-16,
      obj.properties.dir ) end

  end

  map.drawObjects = false

end
```

Then update the enemy's current state and movement, as shown in the following
code:

```
function EnemyUpdate(dt)

  if EnemyDied then

    EnemyDied = false
    --remove the enemy from scene when player kills enemy, scan
      through the table and check if dead == true remove enemy
      table
    for i = #enemyTable, 1, -1 do

      if (enemyTable[i].dead == true) then

        bump.remove(enemyTable[i])

        table.remove(enemyTable, i)


      end
    end
  end


    ---in pairs of i, where v is the value, scan through enemyTable
```

```
for i,v in ipairs(enemyTable) do
    ---and update the displacement velocity vX in particular
       direction dir
    v.vX = (EnemySpeed * v.dir) * dt
    ---get the tiles of the platform
    local vXtile

    --if displacement velocity vX is greater than 0, round the
       left, width and displacement velocity parameters as the
       xTile
    if (v.vX > 0) then vXtile = math.floor((v.l + v.w + v.vX) /
       16)
    --else still roundup anyway, but with the displacement
       velocity less than zero

    else vXtile = math.floor((v.l + v.vX) / 16) end
    --round the top parameter of the enemy gridbox as the yTile
    local yTile = math.floor(v.t / 16) + 1
    ---we have created a bounding to the enemy to know the x and y
       tile that it collides with, now find the tiles in the layer
       of tilemap


    local tile = layer(vXtile, yTile)

    --if the enemy collides on neither of the x or y tiles, change
       direction of motion
    if (tile == nil) then
      v.dir = v.dir * -1
    ---else keep moving, by updating position from left with
       displacement velocity
    else

      v.l = v.l + v.vX

    end
    --let the enemy sprite play animation based on direction

    if (v.dir == 1) then v.animation = EnemyRight
    else v.animation = EnemyLeft end
    --update the animation
    v.animation:update(dt)
  end
end
```

Enemy collision configuration

What happens when the enemy character collides with something (a player or world).

Here, we'll configure the enemy state (dead or alive) based on what it collides with.

```
function collideEnemyWithPlatform(dx,dy,v,obj)

  if obj == player then
  --if the player lands on the top of the enemy character, kill
    enemy

    if (player.t + player.h < v.t + 8) then
      EnemyDie(v)

    else
    --else if the above condition is not met, kill player
      Die()
    end
  end
end
```

Enemy death function

Okay! We've defined in the previous chunks that the enemy can die when the player hits on top of its head. And we have written a few lines of command to destroy the enemy object on the screen. When the enemy death state is set as true, the chunks given here

sets the enemy state as dead whenever the function `EnemyDie()` is called, as shown in the following code:

```
--v holds the properties of the enemy character, so the dead
  Boolean will be set to true whenever the EnemyDie(v) function is
  called.
function EnemyDie(v)
  v.dead = true
  EnemyDied = true
end
```

Drawing the enemy character to the screen

We have defined our enemy character in the previous chunks, but we will now draw it to screen with the following chunk:

```
function DrawEnemy()

    for i,v in ipairs(enemyTable) do
      v.animation:draw(enemyImage, v.l-8,  v.t-16)
    end
end
```

You should call the `DrawEnemy()` function within the `love.draw()` function; if not, it will not display on the screen.

```
function love.draw()
  map:draw()
  DrawPlayer()
  DrawEnemy()
end
```

Finally, add the enemy's bump configuration:

```
--Bump configuration

function bump.collision(obj1, obj2, dx, dy)
  --Bump configuration for player

  if obj1 == player then
    collidePlayerWithPlatform(dx,dy,obj2)
  elseif obj2 == player then
    collidePlayerWithPlatform(-dx,-dy,obj1)
  end
  --Bump configuration for enemy

  for i,v in ipairs(enemyTable) do

    if obj1 == v then
      collideEnemyWithPlatform(dx,dy,v,obj2)
    elseif obj2 == v then
      collideEnemyWithPlatform(-dx,-dy,v,obj1)
    end
  end
end
```

Summary

Now that's all with our enemy character; it can die when a player hits it from the top, and also it moves to and fro like a guard. In the next chapter we will set up game states such as **Game Over**, and create **Head-Up Display** on the screen to update game statistics (life and pickups).

7

Pickups and Head-Up Display and Sounds

We've got our player, enemy, and most of the game all set up, but that's not all. Now we'll be adding pickups (coins and diamonds), and setting up **Head-Up Display (HUD)**, and audio.

Pickups

Let's give the player the task of picking stuff up while it's trying to avoid the antagonists. The pickup items will be in the form of coins and diamonds to reward the player, or up the player's lifespan. And by rewarding the player, we are adding to the player's score. These pickup items include the following:

- Coins
- Diamonds
- Life

Now let's update our `LoadLevel()` function to load our items; we assume we have already added these objects in the Tiled map.

The items enlisted can be loaded into our game code as highlighted in bold text, similar to the way we loaded the player and enemy character inside in the `LoadLevel()` function, as shown in the following code:

```
function LoadLevel(levelFile)
    map = loader.load(levelFile)
    ---fetch gravity property from map
    gravity = map.properties.gravity
    --- set gravity to 1000
    gravity = 1000

    FindSolidTiles(map)
        for i, obj in pairs( map("Objects").objects ) do

        if obj.type == "player" then PlayerSpawn(obj.x,obj.y-8) end
        if obj.type == "enemy" then EnemySpawn(obj.x,obj.y-
           14,obj.properties.dir) end
        ---insert items here
        if obj.type == "diamond" then DiamondSpawn(obj.x,obj.y-16) end
        if obj.type == "coins" then CoinSpawn(obj.x,obj.y-16) end

        if obj.type == "life" then LifeSpawn(obj.x,obj.y-16) end

    end

    map.drawObjects = false

end
```

Items can be drawn and collided on, similar to the way we set up our enemy character; all chunks for the coins, diamonds, and lives are similar.

Coins

We can define the coin parameters and add bump to make it collidable with the player object. When the player collides with the coin, it disappears and we'll update the value for the coins picked on the screen later in this chapter, as shown in the following code:

```
--We'll first set a table to hold the item's bump parameters

CoinTable = {

  l=x,
  t=y,
  w=16,
  h=16
```

```
}
---has the coin been picked? Nah!
local CoinPicked = false
---get the coin image sprite
local CoinImage = love.graphics.newImage("maps/coins.png")
--animate coin, this will make the coin glitter
local a8 = anim8.newGrid(16, 16, CoinImage:getWidth(),
  CoinImage:getHeight())
local CoinGlit = anim8.newAnimation('loop', a8('1-8',1), 0.1)

----set the spawn function and add coin to bump (make it
  collidable)
function CoinSpawn(x,y)
  --for multiple coins display
  local id = #CoinTable+1
  CoinTable[id] = {
    name="coin",
    l=x,

    t=math.floor(y/16)*16+2,
    w=16,
    h=16,

    picked = false

  }
---add coin to bump as static object
  bump.addStatic(CoinTable[id])
end
---now draw coin to screen based on our spawn parameters, that way ---
--they are placed exactly where we want them
function CoinDraw()

  for i,v in ipairs(CoinTable) do
  CoinGlit:draw(CoinImage, v.l, v.t)
  end
end
---the collide callback when player hits the coin, calls CoinPick(v)
which tells that coin picked = true

function collideCoinWithPlatform(dx,dy,v,obj)

  if obj == player then
    CoinPick(v)
  end
end

--- update on the coin's state
```

```
function CoinUpdate(dt)

  if CoinPicked then

     CoinPicked = false
     --remove coin object from screen
     for i = #CoinTable, 1, -1 do
       ---for members of the CoinTable, check if the value of
          picked is set to true, if true then remove coin from
          screen

       if (CoinTable[i].picked == true) then

         bump.remove(CoinTable[i])

         table.remove(CoinTable, i)

       end
     end
  end
--update coin glitter animation
  CoinGlit:update(dt)
end


---function to set coin to true whenever it is called

function CoinPick(v)
  v.picked = true
  CoinPicked = true
end
```

Diamonds

Just as we did with the coins, we'll write very similar code for the diamonds;
we'll create the table that holds the information of the diamonds, animate them,
and also cause the diamonds to disappear when the player collides with them
using the following code:

```
DiamondTable = {
  l=x,
  t=y,
  w=16,
  h=16
}

local DiamondPicked = false
local DiamondImage = love.graphics.newImage("maps/diamonds.png")
```

```
local a8 = anim8.newGrid(16, 16, DiamondImage:getWidth(),
  DiamondImage:getHeight())
local DiamondGlit = anim8.newAnimation('loop', a8('1-4',1), 0.1)
function DiamondSpawn(x,y)
  ----for multiple diamonds to display
  local id = #DiamondTable+1

  DiamondTable[id] = {
    name="diamond",
    l=x,
    t=math.floor(y/16)*16+2,
    w=16,
    h=16,
    picked = false


  }

  bump.addStatic(DiamondTable[id])
end

function DiamondDraw()

  for i,v in ipairs(DiamondTable) do
    DiamondGlit:draw(DiamondImage, v.l, v.t)
  end
end
function collideDiamondWithPlatform(dx,dy,v,obj)

  if obj == player then
    DiamondPick(v)
  end


end
function DiamondUpdate(dt)

  if DiamondPicked then

    DiamondPicked = false

    for i = #DiamondTable, 1, -1 do

      if (DiamondTable[i].picked == true) then

        bump.remove(DiamondTable[i])

        table.remove(DiamondTable, i)

      end
```

```
        end
      end
    DiamondGlit:update(dt)
  end


  function DiamondPick(v)
    v.picked = true
    DiamondPicked = true
  end
```

Life

Every object to be picked in the game world has the same code with few edits; the chunks for the life are no different from the diamonds' and coins' chunks. But in this case we are not using a sprite for the life stash, so we wouldn't need to declare quads.

```
LifeTable = {
  l=x,
  t=y,
  w=16,
  h=16
}

local LifePicked = false
local LifeImage = love.graphics.newImage("maps/life.png")

function LifeSpawn(x,y)

  local id = #LifeTable+1

  LifeTable[id] = {
    name="life",
    l=x,
    t=math.floor(y/16)*16+2,
    w=16,
    h=16,
    picked = false

  }

  bump.addStatic(LifeTable[id])
```

```
end

function LifeDraw()

  for i,v in ipairs(LifeTable) do
    love.graphics.drawq(LifeImage, v.l, v.t)
  end
end
function collideLifeWithPlatform(dx,dy,v,obj)

  if obj == player then
    LifePick(v)
  end


end
function LifeUpdate(dt)

  if LifePicked then

    LifePicked = false

    for i = #LifeTable, 1, -1 do

      if (LifeTable[i].picked == true) then

        bump.remove(LifeTable[i])

        table.remove(LifeTable, i)

      end
    end
  end
end


function LifePick(v)
  v.picked = true
  LifePicked = true
end
```

We can now get LÖVE to draw the items, update them, and add them to the bump configuration as shown in the following code:

```
--Update them
function love.update(dt)
   bump.collide()
   PlayerMovement(dt)
   EnemyUpdate(dt)
   CoinUpdate(dt)
   DiamondUpdate(dt)
   LifeUpdate(dt)
end

--Draw them

function love.draw()

   map:draw()

   DrawPlayer()

   DrawEnemy()
   CoinDraw()
   DiamondDraw()
   LifeDraw()
end

--Bump configuration

function bump.collision(obj1, obj2, dx, dy)
   --Bump configuration for player

   if obj1 == player then
     collidePlayerWithPlatform(dx,dy,obj2)
   elseif obj2 == player then
     collidePlayerWithPlatform(-dx,-dy,obj1)
   end
   --Bump configuration for enemy

   for i,v in ipairs(enemyTable) do

     if obj1 == v then
       collideEnemyWithPlatform(dx,dy,v,obj2)
     elseif obj2 == v then
       collideEnemyWithPlatform(-dx,-dy,v,obj1)
     end
   end

   --Bump configuration for Coin
```

```
      for i,v in ipairs(CoinTable) do
        if obj1 == v then
          collideCoinWithPlatform(dx,dy,v,obj2)
        elseif obj2 == v then
          collideCoinWithPlatform(-dx,-dy,v,obj1)
        end
      end

      --Bump configuration for Diamond

      for i,v in ipairs(DiamondTable) do
        if obj1 == v then
          collideDiamondWithPlatform(dx,dy,v,obj2)
        elseif obj2 == v then
          collideDiamondWithPlatform(-dx,-dy,v,obj1)
        end
      end
      --Bump configuration Life
      for i,v in ipairs(LifeTable) do
        if obj1 == v then
          collideLifeWithPlatform(dx,dy,v,obj2)
        elseif obj2 == v then
          collideLifeWithPlatform(-dx,-dy,v,obj1)
        end
      end
    end
```

Finally, we are done with characters and pickups; we can now go on and add audio to our game. To do this, we are going to leverage LÖVE's inbuilt audio system.

Audio system

LÖVE leverages OpenAL for audio playback; it provides the `love.audio` module that uses only one type of object, a source file. It's simple to use, and wherever the callback `love.audio.play()` is put in a function, it plays the sound.

```
    ---fetch the audio file from source

    BgSound = love.audio.newSource("bgsound.mp3", "stream")
    --set the volume of the sound
    BgSound:setVolume(0.5)
    --set the pitch level
    BgSound:setPitch(0.25)
    --play the sound, you can also use shorthand BgSound:play()
    love.audio.play(BgSound)
```

What we have done so far is to fetch the audio file to be played from source, set the volume and pitch, and then play it. In this case, the sound will stream from the disk compressed, unless it's specified as `static`. `Static` is good for short sound in which the sound is loaded into the memory; but for our background music, the sound will probably be long. So, we'll not use static but use stream, which means the sound will stream from disk without loading into memory first.

Enemy collision sounds

We are going to play a sound whenever the enemy hits the player or vice-versa, so we set a hit sound and its volume and pitch properties in the code below:

```
--here we make the sound static
HitSound = love.audio.newSource("hit.mp3", "static")
--set volume and pitch
HitSound:setVolume(0.75)

HitSound:setPitch(0.5)
```

To play the hit sound when enemy collides with player or vice-versa, we'll call HitSound:play() in the CollideEnemyWithPlatform() function:

```
function collideEnemyWithPlatform(dx,dy,v,obj)

  if obj == player then
  --if the player lands on the top of the enemy character, kill
    enemy
    if (player.t + player.h < v.t + 2) then
      EnemyDie(v)
      HitSound:play()
    else
  --else if the above condition is not met, kill player
      Die()
      HitSound:play()
    end
  end
end
```

Item pick sounds

Now we can now place `PickupSound:play()` by updating the `CollideCoinWithPlatform()`, `CollideLifeWithPlatform()` and `CollideDiamondWithPlatform()` functions as we did with the enemy-player collide function.

```
PickupSound = love.audio.newSource("pickup.mp3", "static")
PickupSound:setVolume(0.5)
PickupSound:setPitch(0.25)
```

Coin sound

When a player collides with a coin, the coin will disappear and `PickupSound:play()` will play the sound, as shown in the following code:

```
function collideCoinWithPlatform(dx,dy,v,obj)
  if obj == player then
    CoinPick(v)
    ---play sound
    PickupSound:play()
  end
end
Life sound
```

Diamond sound

When a player collides with a diamond, the coin will disappear and `PickupSound:play()` will play the sound, as shown in the following code:

```
function collideDiamondWithPlatform(dx,dy,v,obj)

  if obj == player then
    DiamondPick(v)
    ---play sound
    PickupSound:play()
  end
end
```

That's it about audio, `PickupSound:play()`. Make sure the audio files exist in the source folder of your game project, in order to be assured that the sounds will play when required.

Head-Up Display (HUD)

The HUD can be described as the graphical interface for displaying the game information such as life stat, player score, and so on.

Menu HUD

Here we'll simply create a "Start Game" and "Quit Game" button with text, but before we do that we have to set up game states— a type of state machine that tells the various modes of a game whether the game is at the menu mode or is currently playing (game-play mode).

In the `love.load()` function, set a game state as menu, so whenever the game loads its first state is the menu.

```
function love.load()
gamestate = "menu"
love.graphics.setBackgroundColor(225, 153, 0)
-- load the level and bind the variable map
  LoadTileMap("tilemap.tmx")
end
```

Next, we are setting another `gamestate` condition; game should update and draw only when game state is `"playing"`:

```
--Update them
function love.update(dt)
  if gamestate == "playing" then
    bump.collide()
    PlayerMovement(dt)
    EnemyUpdate(dt)
    CoinUpdate(dt)
    DiamondUpdate(dt)
    LifeUpdate(dt)
  end
end

--Draw them

function love.draw()

  if gamestate == "playing" then

    map:draw()
```

```
        DrawPlayer()

        DrawEnemy()
        CoinDraw()
        DiamondDraw()
        LifeDraw()
    end
  end
```

The game will only draw and update when game state is set as `"playing"`. So in the `"menu"` game state, we'll setup our menu texts and functions, so menu functions will only work in the `"menu"` game state.

Let's create a table to hold our button properties, the x position, y position, the text to be displayed, and the identity of the text.

```
button = {}
function ButtonSpawn(x, y, text, id)
    table.insert(button, {x=x, y=y, text=text, mouseover=false})
end
```

We can go on and insert the `ButtonSpawn()` function inside the `love.load` function, so we can load the particular text that will represent our button.

```
function love.load()
gamestate = "menu"
love.graphics.setBackgroundColor(225, 153, 0)
-- load the level and bind the variable map
  LoadTileMap("tilemap.tmx")
-- load the buttons
  ButtonSpawn(300, 200, "START GAME", "start")
  ButtonSpawn(300, 300, "QUIT GAME", "quit")
end
```

Before the button will be displayed on the screen, it is a tradition that we have to draw it. `ButtonDraw()` must be called in the `love.draw` function.

Put `medium = love.graphics.newFont(45)` inside `love.load`, to load the font size then, as shown in the following code:

```
function ButtonDraw()
   for i, v in ipairs(button) do
   ---if mouse is not on button, the color should be black
   if v.mousover == false then
      love.graphics.setColor(0,0,0)
   end


   ---if mouse is on button


   if v.mousover == true then
      love.graphics.setColor(0,252,252)
   end


   love.graphics.setFont(medium)
   love.graphics.print(v.text, v.x, v.y)
end
```

On clicking a button

We need the button to react to the mouse click; when you click a button it should do something. That is what we will achieve with the `ButtonClick()` function:

```
function ButtonClick(x, y)
   for i, v in ipairs(button) do
      ---if the mouse is within the button
      if x > v.x and x < v.x + medium:getWidth(v.text) and y > v.y
         and y < v.y+medium:getHeight(v.text) then
         ---if the id of the button clicked is quit, then exit game

         if v.id == "quit" then
            love.event.push("quit")
         end
         ---if the id of the button clicked is Start, set gamestate =
            "playing"
         if v.id == "start" then
            gamestate = "playing"
         end
      end
   end
end


   ----if the mouse is clicked at certain coordinates x,y
```

```
function love.mouspressed(x,y)
  ---be sure we are in the menu game state

  if gamestate == "menu" then

    ButtonClick(x,y)

  end

end
```

Let's check if the mouse is on the button or not, so we'll set `mouseover` as
`true` or `false`.

```
function MouseCheck()
  for i, v in ipairs(button) do
  ---if the mouse is within the button
    if mousex > v.x and mousex < v.x +  medium:getWidth(v.text)
      and mousey > v.y and mousey < v.y+medium:getHeight(v.text)
      then
      v.mouseover = true
    else
      v.mouseover = false
    end
  end
end
```

Now update the function `love.update` to hold `MouseCheck()`, whenever the game
state is `"menu"`.

```
--Update them
function love.update(dt)
  if gamestate == "menu" then
    MenuCheck()
  end
  if gamestate == "playing" then
    bump.collide()
    PlayerMovement(dt)
    EnemyUpdate(dt)
    CoinUpdate(dt)
    DiamondUpdate(dt)
    LifeUpdate(dt)
  end
end
```

That's it about buttons!

Life HUD

The life HUD will display the number of lives the player has left. We'll just do simple math to add life when a player collides with the life item, and subtract it when a player dies.

```
local life = 3
```

When a player hits the life item, the calculations are as follows:

```
life = life + 1
```

When s player dies, the calculations are as follows:

```
life = life - 1
```

Print the life count on screen using the following code:

```
love.graphics.print("Life: " life, 32, 32)
love.graphics.setFont(medium)
```

Now let's insert this into our main chunk:

```
life = 3
---when player picks life item
function LifePick(v)
  v.picked = true
  LifePicked = true

  lifebar = lifebar + 1

end
```
Now when player dies, update the Die() function:
```
---for now make the player re-spawn to position 32,32 on the tilemap
when it dies.

function Die()

  life = life - 1

  player.l = 32

  player.t = 32
end
```

Score HUD

Whenever a player hits a coin, kills a player, or picks a diamond, we would need to increase their score by 50, 100, and 150 respectively.

```
local score = 100
---when player picks coin
function CoinPick(v)
  v.picked = true
  CoinPicked = true

  score = score + 50

end
---when player picks coin
function DiamondPick(v)
  v.picked = true
  DiamondPicked = true

  score = score + 150

end
---when player kills enemy score 100, else remove 100
function collideEnemyWithPlatform(dx,dy,v,obj)
  if obj == player then
    if (player.t + player.h < v.t + 2) then
      EnemyDie(v)
      Score = score + 100
    else
      Die()
      Score = score - 100
    end
  end


end
```

We can now update the love.draw function to print the Life and Score on the screen:

```
function love.draw()

  if gamestate == "playing" then

    love.graphics.print("Life:"..life, 32, 32)
```

```
        love.graphics.print("Score:"..score, 320, 32)

        love.graphics.setFont(medium)

        map:draw()

        DrawPlayer()

        DrawEnemy()
        CoinDraw()
        DiamondDraw()
        LifeDraw()
    end
end
```

Summary

Finally! We are done with all the game logic, we have a full game level already, and from here you can create as many levels as you want using the same method you used to create the first one! In the next chapter we'll learn how to package/compile our games in distributable formats for PC, Linux, and Mac.

8
Packaging and Distributing Your Game

We've developed our game and are ready to distribute it. Traditionally, the contents of the root folder (make sure the `main.lua` file is in the root folder.) of the game should be zipped and renamed with a `.love` extension. With that, our game will play because LÖVE is already installed on our development computer. But when we distribute our game, we do not expect the users or gamers to already have LÖVE installed on their computers. For PC and Mac users, we'll have to distribute the game in `.exe` and `.app` formats respectively.

Windows executable

The process of creating an executable format of our game is very easy by following the given steps:

1. Download the source folder of LÖVE by visiting `love2d.org` and click on **Zipped 32-bit**.

2. Extract the folder, copy the `love.exe` file in there together with our game's `.love` file, and put both of them in another folder (for example, `My game`)

3. Press Window key + *R*. In the panel displayed, type `cmd` and click on **Run**, a console will display on the screen.

4. Now enter the following command: `cd [directory to our game]`. For example, on my computer, the `My game` folder is stored in `My Documents` folder. My command line will look like the following command:

   `cd c:/users/DarmieAkinlaja/My Documents/My game`

5. Then you can now append your game .love file with the love.exe file, and create your desired executable file by entering the following command line:

```
copy /b love.exe+mygame.love mygame.exe
```

6. Immediately after you press the Enter button, an .exe version of your game will be created in the same folder (My game) where you placed the love.exe and mygame.love files.

7. Copy the resulting mygame.exe file and all the .dll files you find in the downloaded LÖVE source zip, and package them in another folder (the folder you wish to distribute your executable game with must have these .dll files to work)

8. You are good to go!

Mac apps

Once you have your game prepared as .love file, you can make your game available for Mac OS X users by using the official LÖVE Zipped Universal Build from love2d.org. This is a straightforward approach just as with the windows executable. Follow the given steps:

1. Unzip the Zipped Universal Build.

2. Rename the love.app as mygame.app.

3. Copy the .love file of your packed game (mygame.love) into mygame.app/Contents/Resources.

4. Modify mygame.app/Contents/info.plist by changing org.love2d.love to com.mycompany.mygame under CFBundleIdentifier, and change Löve to mygame under CFBundleName. Then remove the following section:

```
<key>UTExportedTypeDeclarations</key>
<array>
    . . .
</array>
```

5. Now zip your mygame.app folder (for example, mygame.osx.zip), and distribute it.

6. You are good to go!

mygame should be replaced with whatever name you give your game, and should be written without spaces. And mycompany should be replaced with whatever name you choose for your company, to be written without spaces.

Linux

Linux operating systems will run .love directly without having to package it into special extension. Just compress your game source folder as .zip and rename the extension as .love; you are good to go! This is because, as of writing, those managing LÖVE haven't figured out a way of packaging to specific Linux distribution.

LÖVE on browsers

As of writing, this is still an experimental project; it will allow your LÖVE game to play directly in a WebGL-supported browser without extra plugins. More information on this can be found at https://love2d.org/forums/viewtopic.php?f=5&t=8487.

LÖVE on Android mobile phones

This too is an experiment and not yet perfected. Its support is limited as there are some features of your game that will probably not work. But you can follow up on this project at https://love2d.org/forums/viewforum.php?f=11.

Summary

Awesome! That's it! We just designed a video game from scratch to finish! We learned from the first chapter to the last how to produce a video game with the LÖVE framework. Now you can distribute your games to stores and make some cash while you entertain your players. Have Fun!

Index

diamond 32
executable format, creating 83, 84
isometric view, URL 25
planning 25, 26
player 32
role-playing game 26
side-scrolling, URL 25
simulation 26
strategy 26

W

Windows
  executable 83, 84
Windows users
  LÖVE, downloading for 8

Thank you for buying
LÖVE for Lua Game Programming

About Packt Publishing

Packt, pronounced 'packed', published its first book "*Mastering phpMyAdmin for Effective MySQL Management*" in April 2004 and subsequently continued to specialize in publishing highly focused books on specific technologies and solutions.

Our books and publications share the experiences of your fellow IT professionals in adapting and customizing today's systems, applications, and frameworks. Our solution based books give you the knowledge and power to customize the software and technologies you're using to get the job done. Packt books are more specific and less general than the IT books you have seen in the past. Our unique business model allows us to bring you more focused information, giving you more of what you need to know, and less of what you don't.

Packt is a modern, yet unique publishing company, which focuses on producing quality, cutting-edge books for communities of developers, administrators, and newbies alike. For more information, please visit our website: www.packtpub.com.

About Packt Open Source

In 2010, Packt launched two new brands, Packt Open Source and Packt Enterprise, in order to continue its focus on specialization. This book is part of the Packt Open Source brand, home to books published on software built around Open Source licences, and offering information to anybody from advanced developers to budding web designers. The Open Source brand also runs Packt's Open Source Royalty Scheme, by which Packt gives a royalty to each Open Source project about whose software a book is sold.

Writing for Packt

We welcome all inquiries from people who are interested in authoring. Book proposals should be sent to author@packtpub.com. If your book idea is still at an early stage and you would like to discuss it first before writing a formal book proposal, contact us; one of our commissioning editors will get in touch with you.

We're not just looking for published authors; if you have strong technical skills but no writing experience, our experienced editors can help you develop a writing career, or simply get some additional reward for your expertise.

XNA 4.0 Game Development by Example – Visual Basic Edition

Create your own exciting games with Visual Basic and Microsoft XNA 4.0

Beginner's Guide

Kurt Jaegers

XNA 4.0 Game Development by Example: Beginner's Guide – Visual Basic Edition

ISBN: 978-1-84969-240-3   Paperback: 424 pages

Create your own exciting games with Visual Basic and Microsoft XNA 4.0

1. Dive headfirst into game creation with Visual Basic and the XNA Framework

2. Four different styles of games comprising a puzzler, space shooter, multi-axis shoot 'em up, and a jump-and-run platformer

3. Packed with many suggestions for expanding your finished game that will make you think critically, technically, and creatively.

Corona SDK Mobile Game Development

Create monetized games for iOS and Android with minimum cost and code

Beginner's Guide

Michelle M. Fernandez

Corona SDK Mobile Game Development: Beginner's Guide

ISBN: 978-1-84969-188-8   Paperback: 408 pages

Create monetized games for iOS and Android with minimum cost and code

1. Build once and deploy your games to both iOS and Android

2. Create commercially successful games by applying several monetization techniques and tools

3. Create three fun games and integrate them with social networks such as Twitter and Facebook

Please check **www.PacktPub.com** for information on our titles

SDL Game Development

ISBN: 978-1-84969-682-1   Paperback: 256 pages

Discover how to leverage the power of SDL 2.0 to create awesome games in C++

1. Create 2D reusable games using the new SDL 2.0 and C++ frameworks

2. Become proficient in speeding up development time

3. Create two fully-featured games with C++ which include a platform game and a 2D side scrolling shooter

Cocos2d-X by Example Beginner's Guide

ISBN: 978-1-78216-734-1   Paperback: 246 pages

Make fun games for any platform using C++, combined with one of the most popular open source frameworks in the world

1. Learn to build multi-device games in simple, easy steps, letting the framework do all the heavy lifting

2. Spice things up in your games with easy to apply animations, particle effects, and physics simulation

3. Quickly implement and test your own gameplay ideas, with an eye for optimization and portability

Please check **www.PacktPub.com** for information on our titles